D1168856

Arrivals

Poems by David Mason

Story Line Press
2004

Published by Story Line Press
Three Oaks Farm
PO Box 1240, Ashland, Oregon 97520-0055
www.storylinepress.com

This publication was made possible thanks in part to
the generous support of our individual contributors.

Cover and author photographs by Anne Lennox
Book design by Sharon McCann

Library of Congress Cataloging-in-Publication Data

Mason, David, 1954–
Arrivals / poems by David Mason.
p. cm.
ISBN 1-58654-036-X
I. Title.
PS3563.A7879A88 2004
811'.54--dc22
2004001081

In memory of my father
James Cameron Mason
1921–2003

CONTENTS

I
The Dream of Arrival

11 The City
12 In Transit
13 Gulls in the Wake
14 Schoolchildren at Mistras
15 On the Terrace
17 Kalamitsi
18 Acrostic from Aegina
19 Pelicans and Greeks
21 Mumbai
22 A Beggar of Chennai
23 Towers of Silence
24 The Chambered Cairn
25 Limerick Junction
27 New Zealand Letter
31 *Agnostos Topos*
33 The Dream of Arrival

II
The Collector's Tale

37 The Collector's Tale

III
In the Borrowed House

47 In the Borrowed House
48 The Session
49 Adam Speaks
50 Night Squall
51 *Mise en Scène*
52 Ballade at 3 AM
53 Small Steps

IV

Swimmers on the Shore

59   A Meaning Made of Trees

60   The Lost House

61   The Picketwire

62   A Mountain Saxifrage

63   A Birthday

66   Mr. Louden and the Antelope

67   A Dance in Desolation Sound

70   Winter 1963

72   Swimmers on the Shore

74   A Float

Notes

Acknowledgments

About the Author

❧ I ❧

The Dream of Arrival

THE CITY
after the Greek of C. P. Cavafy

You said: "I'll go away to another shore,
find another city better than this.
In all I attempt, something remains amiss
and my heart—like a dead thing—lies buried.
How long will my mind stew in all its worry?
Wherever I cast my eye, wherever I look,
I see the ruins of my life turn black
here where I wasted and wrecked many a year."

You won't find a new land or another shore.
This city will follow you, you'll molder
in these streets, in these neighborhoods grow older,
and turn gray among familiar houses.
You'll always end here—don't hope for other places—
there is no ship, there is no road for you.
Now that you have decided you are through
with this place, you've wrecked your life everywhere.

IN TRANSIT

The urge to settle never stays for long,
nor does desire to move like a windblown seed
when days have no more purpose than a song
at midnight, drifting from the olive trees,
or books you packed but cannot seem to read.
The passing stranger is well-known in Greece.

Once in Athens you rode the crowded bus,
watching the dull eyes of those who aimed for work
through gritty streets, the traffic's heave and thrust.
Elsewhere the perfect sculpture of the light
reminded you what leaves us in the dark.
No Baedeker explained your jaded sight.

Islands, more islands than you could name,
lay like lovers at morning: *Don't leave. Stay.*
But the only Eden that could ever claim
you wholly disappeared beneath the waves.
Revise, tomorrow, what you write today,
as tides reform in mouths of the sea caves.

A fisherman's fantasy, after all—
sun-dazed, wine-dazed—with a flick of her fins
dives out of sight, ignoring his fervent call
while his boat nods *yes* on the dancing sea.
Here all the turmoil of desire begins.
You are as happy as you'll ever be.

GULLS IN THE WAKE

Late in our journey from the pier at Kos
I had come up for air. Most passengers
had found their bunks or drunk themselves asleep
in the comfy bar. Adrift and floodlit,

I let suspended time wash over me,
its kitchen smells, salt wind and plodding engines,
as two guys swinging beer cans walked the deck,
singing the liturgy. *Christ is risen!*

Drunken, genuinely happy, they waved
across cool space at constellated lights
of villages, and greeted me, a stranger.
I answered, *Truly He is risen,* though

I don't believe it. Not risen for this world.
Not here. Not now.
                              Then I heard cadences
of priestly chanting from an Athens church
broadcast to any pilgrim still awake.

Who could explain an unbeliever's joy
as rockets flared from the coast near Sounion
and music ferried death to life out there,
untethered in the dark?

And that was when I saw them—ghostly, winged,
doggedly following outside our light,
hopeful without a thought of hope, feeding
and diving to feed in waves I could not see.

SCHOOLCHILDREN AT MISTRAS

Snow falls above the smoky vale of Sparta
in mountains where the weak were once abandoned.
Everywhere you turn, the old world is unearthed
between the shops where citizens still wait
for a change of season, or, outside of town,
gather the olives, crate the winter oranges.

A hush ascends the ruined holy city
from the stare of Christ to battlements above,
from the nun who leads her three goats out to grass
and almond trees that blossom another snow—
silence these schoolchildren happily shatter,
as if escaping death in the museum.

ON THE TERRACE

High on resinous wine,
we watch the light grow redder.
A neighboring shepherd's son
trundles a load of fodder

deep into shade and sits,
as patient as the day,
deaf to his father's fits—
he knows how to make hay.

And we make conversation,
our friends and you and I,
ample compensation
under an azure sky.

Below, the crooked spines
of village rooftops reach
to the horizon's lines:
the sun-struck hills, the beach,

and the straight line of the sea
that is not a line at all
but much like your mystery
holding me in thrall.

The evening stills. An owl
perches on nearby tiles,
matronly, comical,
ignoring our drunken smiles.

Her mate lands at her tail
and old tile rooftops clatter.
She puts up such a wail
we wonder what's the matter.

But it's only love, we see,
or instinct for the chase.
You look across at me—
a look I can't erase

because I'll never know
if it was love or hate.
Now time begins to slow
and I can't concentrate.

Our laughter dies with the light.
The owls and friends depart.
Decades have taken flight,
and we were wrong from the start.

KALAMITSI

A path I had not walked for sixteen years,
now almost hidden under rain-soaked grass
so even the locals told me it was gone,
but two steps down where it rounded the bay
and I was back. My heart beat all the faster.

Though half the olive trees had been cut down
the stone wall stood, the gate, the little house
looking as if no one ever lived there,
the cool spring where I dipped a pot for water
hidden by bramble mounds, the cistern greening.

I stiffly climbed the gate (now chained and locked)
and walked the point of land and knew each tree—
nothing but private memories, after all.
It wasn't the loss of time or friends that moved me
but the small survivals I was here to mark.

I had come through to see this much again,
and that plank bench under a cypress tree
where I had placed it all those years ago
to soak up shade on summer afternoons—
only a small plank bench, but quite enough.

ACROSTIC FROM AEGINA

Anemones you brought back from the path
Nod in a glass beside our rumpled bed.
Now you are far away. In the aftermath
Even these flowers arouse my sleepy head.

Love, when I think of the ready look in your eyes,
Erotas that would make these stone walls blush
Nerves me to write away the morning's hush.
Nadir of longing, and the red anemones
Over the lucent rim—my poor designs,
X-rated praise I've hidden between these lines.

PELICANS AND GREEKS
Edward Lear in San Remo, Italy, 1888

Nights when he cannot sleep, Lear looks for paper,
uncertain whether he should sketch or write,
or which of his living friends might comprehend
his travels off the rough and tumble roads.

As soon as I picked up my pen I felt
I was dying.

                And should he then have married?
On such long nights, lines from the Laureate
chase through his brain like notes flung off the scale—
an infant *with no language but a cry....*

What of Bassaë, the temple on the mountain,
the ancient oaks still stretching out their arms
to sunlight he had tried to catch in oils?
Who owned that painting now? How could one own
the love that lay behind it? All the years
and all the travels must mean little more
than light that dies along the temple flutings.

Laden with lunch, the drawing boards and paints,
Georgis played Sancho Panza to his knight.
Dear Georgis—you who witnessed wonders with me....
Spoken to nothing but an empty room.

On Crete a black man came, and little boy,
and peasants, and I drew them. They were all
good tempered, laughing. I remember how
the small boy saw my drawing of a donkey
and almost cried and was impelled to give me
lemons as a gift. I gave him a pencil.
A gesture I can't forget, ingenuous

and awkward like the play of pelicans—
the ordinary beauty of the world
that makes one jubilate in sheer delight
and shudder when we feel life leaving us.

In India an English schoolgirl came
to meet the painter, having memorized
"The Owl and the Pussycat." Such was fame.
And there was Georgis who was mad again
because he could not ride an elephant.
And there were mountains higher than the ones
he loved in Crete and Thessaly. They too
compelled the draughtsman's longing not to lose
minute sensations he had drawn upon,
fleabags and palaces, pelicans and Greeks.

If no one bought my drawings I should live
on figs in summertime, worms in winter,
with olive trees and onions, a parrot,
yes, and two hedgehogs for companionship,
a painting room with absolute north light....

So many friends are gone. No partner frets
that he cannot sleep, no child arrives to scold him.
He is the sum of all that he has lost,
his hand still dreaming on the empty page.

MUMBAI

The crowd's no apparition on Nehru Road,
nor the grit of motor rickshaws on Nehru Road.

Nor the steady pace of people, raga, rock,
and all the unheard music of Nehru Road.

Nor the flowers, the fruit, bowls of sacred colors,
the goats and cows that stroll down Nehru Road.

The tiffinwallahs, Internet cafes,
the dogs that lick the pavement of Nehru Road.

The girls with perfect skin who wear their saris
with a demigoddess air on Nehru Road.

The crones who squat, the beggars, and the boy
washing himself from a pail on Nehru Road.

Commuters lean for air from open doors
as the long train leaves the stop on Nehru Road.

Mason, you've come to the other side of the world—
why can't you lose yourself on Nehru Road?

A BEGGAR OF CHENNAI

What roll of the dice made me the healthy one
placing a rupee on his left arm's stump?
I watched him flip the coin from the bone knob
into his mouth with a rueful little laugh
at his own predicament, then beg for more.

Whether it was karma or chaos that parted us,
I drove away with friends in a hotel car.
But I was followed by the flattened look
of the armless boy, who eyed the airport crowd
as if in full acceptance of a gambling god.

Soon Chennai traffic heaved from all directions—
foot or bullock, bus or motor rickshaw—
headlong, woven by invisible hands
so multiple I could not count the strands.

Limbo of airports, and a world traversed
at jet speed, jammed in with others, waited on.
Day and night are reversed, but even in
the Lariam dream of India you find
familiar Coke signs next to temple walls—
no one escapes the multinationals.

Along the river sacred to a god
there is much to be transcended, like the smell
of shit that rises from a shanty town,
the oily campfires of the hacking poor
and barefoot children picking through the trash.
Everything's recycled. Every life is short.

Even in Malabar, haven of the rich
where endless traffic lurches toward the light
of Marine Drive, you pass the wooded hill
well known for Parsi rituals of death,
the loved one's body given to the birds
that congregate upon the tower grounds.

And after feasting on such well-fed flesh
these same birds might appear in photographs
of unsuspecting tourists like yourself,
or sail with equanimity above
commuter trains, apartment blocks, hotels—
all places of a temporary shelter.

You are not here for long.
The city unreels like a plotless movie
screened in a taxi window, yet you breathe
the same bad air as beggars and moguls.
Passing the hillside where the towers stand,
you sweat without AC and do not chatter.

THE CHAMBERED CAIRN
For Anne Lennox

Kilbirnie's kirkyard and the lairs at Largs
muffle their hauntings in the greenest lawn.
A line of houses known as Daisybank
stands by the Garnock, which is not so pure
as it once was, though a gray heron homes there.

And gray your father's cousin, ninety-three.
Alert, rail-thin, stone deaf but talkative,
he sways in his armchair while his bony hands
jab and slice tall tales. His false teeth whistle,
his old eyes water, *whether I laugh or no.*

Gray too your aunt who tholes atop the brae,
mean in poverty, stunted as a child.
The Home Help come in aprons to make tea
and plead with her to leave her moldy walls.
She sits beside her window, judging neighbors.

What makes the old man happy with his lot,
the aunt a limping harpy of complaint,
you do not know, though you would aid them both.
Thinking Ayrshire, speaking American,
you cannot even say where you belong,

the family broken like a chambered cairn
you found on Arran—what's left a mound of grass
and a few skewed stones to mark the burials,
secrets kept from the archeologist.
None lives who can name the dead of that place

with its raided passage aimed at Ailsa Craig.

LIMERICK JUNCTION

Thick smoke in the train from Dublin
as raucous boys carouse
calls back my youth in the sixties
and how we used to grouse,

dissing the war, our parents,
the system and all that stuff.
How could it seem so long ago
yet hardly long enough?

I contemplate the haze,
green Ireland passing by,
above it the slow, evolving
still point of the sky.

Here to teach a fortnight,
I turn a thin book's pages,
as if each leaf I fumble
were a day the traveler ages.

Receipts and ticket stubs
bulge from my tweed pocket.
The kid with the joint in his mouth
sports a leather jacket

in homage to some Brando
his generation knows.
Nearing Limerick Junction,
the train car groans and slows.

The boys pile out for Limerick
while I'm off to Tralee.
I breathe the last illegal smoke
and settle for hot tea.

It has begun to rain.
The future at my back,
I'll read some more of that slender book
and trust the rusting track.

NEW ZEALAND LETTER
For Anne Stevenson and Peter Lucas

"Nothing, not even the wind that blows, is so unstable
as the level of the crust of the earth." – Charles Darwin

This morning, groggy and a bit footsore
from another tramp in these New Zealand hills,
I write to you, Anne and Peter, in Wales
or Durham, no doubt hoofing it yourselves—
or Anne with Mozart at her fingertips,
Peter tracking Darwin across the page.
Just now the sun slipped under laden clouds,
lighting a forest that, from where I sit,
could be some alternate Seattle, made
by an artist fond of hobbits and Maori lore,
exotic but expected like the sky
two nights ago: Orion on his back,
and at the opposite end what Bishop called
the kite sticks of the Southern Cross.

                              Out here
in Queenstown's alps I'm slightly less at sea.
Two weeks ago, in a Northland port of call
that battened down its hatches while a squall
unsteadied solid earth like a tipped canoe,
I lay for hours awake on Hospital Hill
in a rented room, my Anne asleep beside me.
The continent of home, familiar, firm,
was far away. I felt, as Freud might say,
that oceanic, vague, religious sense,
my confirmation of insignificance,
and wondered with my hearing aids turned off
how thought would swim if I were totally deaf,
if wind and sails, wails, whales, and even Wales,
were all the same descending sonar ping,
an undersea sensation. I thought of friends
like you who sound these depths without the bends.

Forgive this letter from a wanderer.
My mind panning, a fluid Steadicam,
I've moved (with Annie) out of that bed
and that original, subversive storm,
afoot, entrained, by bus, in a small plane
I feared a gale would dash like a beer can
against a mountain's wall of woods—in short
like Willie Nelson "On the road again,"
albeit in this tenuous sea-land,
the haven of environmentalists.
Forgive the *sound* of this, my sounding out
locations you have yet to see or hear,
and let me tender my small vision here.

Begin with the region's young geology,
the accident of islands that still rise
and spiral into zig-zag mountain ranges,
glaciers long and white as wizards' beards,
cold rivers, silt green or so transparent
they flow like breezes blowing over stones.
Now fill in lichens, mosses, undergrowth
of silver fern and berry-laden shrubs,
the eerie forest of the podocarp,
its leafless branches choked by hanging moss,
rare stands of rimu pine, the nikau palm,
sheep meadows scoured by European gorse—
alpine, tropical and imported plants
tossed on the rumps and hummocks of the land
right down to the shoreline birds, the dotterels,
whimbrels, bar-tailed godwits, white-faced heron
lording like headwaiters at low tide,
the shags and oystercatchers, penguins, grebes.
And here the albatross alights at last,
world traveler folding its weary wings.
Inland, white-backed magpies and pokeko birds

dot meadows, while in woods the begging wekas
pester walkers. Others I need hearing aids
to catch: fantails, bellbirds, twitching finches
chatter in humid shade, guarding their eggs
from possums or the poisons humans spray.

Which brings me around at last to swelling towns
like Auckland, Napier, Christchurch, Wellington,
the tourist hustle, some of it rough as guts,
where Poms and Yanks, Pakehas of all stripes,
mix with Maori and new wave immigrants,
fractious and varied as the forest birds.
It's like Creation's proud Cloudcuckooland
but earthbound, addled by bungy-jumping youth.
Each permanent or momentary claim
asserts a version of this land and sea
so freshly robbed of its virginity,
where moko hoons mark turf, spray-painting walls,
or clash like rugby teams in free-for-alls.
The spillage of spoiled empires everywhere
rumbles ashore like the redundant surf.

Yet the never-far-off sea still models change
like that wind I started with, to rearrange
Aoteroa, land of the white cloud.
Darwin hated it and only stayed
a week, bound for the sedentary life
that would explore as no one else had done
currents in all species known to the sun.
And terminal cases on every kind of pill
in every weather out on Hospital Hill
can try to see the earth for what it is,
not as the perfect dream that always dies,
the Promised Land promoted in brochures,
but as the sort of matter that endures

by changing. Some of its forms we recognize;
others astonish—the inarticulate
we try to voice before it is too late,
this metamorphic world, tidal and worn,
rooted, adrift, alive, and dying to be born.

We had walked a whole day on high ridges
somewhere between the heat-struck sea and peaks,
each breath a desert in a traveler's lungs,
salt-stung, dusty, like summer's rasping grass
and the roughness of stone. Biblical thorns
penned us, while the stunted ilex trees
shadowed the path. It seemed from these dour fields
we could not emerge on anything like a road.

A landscape no one had commodified
or fenced. If there were gardens here
the poverty of soil defeated them.
If there were homes beyond some goatherd's hut
the gravity of ages pulled them down.
No sound but cicadas like high-pitched drills
ringing till red sunlight hissed into the sea.

And that was when, our shins scratched and throats
        parched,
we stumbled into a village on the shore
where people, stupefied by days upon days
that were the same, told us what to call this place.
The distance to a road? *Two cigarettes,*
said the old man who sat webbing his net.

Now the road cuts down from the cliffs above.
I've been back, bought wine from the old man's son
who keeps his car parked in an olive's shade.
It's better, of course, that one can come and go.
One needn't stare a lifetime at hot cliffs,
thinking them impassable except to goats
and men whose speech and features grew like thorns.

The old man's dead. The friends I traveled with
are long since out of touch, and I'll admit
I've lost much of a young man's nimbleness.
I call these passing years *agnostos topos,*
unknown country, a place of panting lizards.
Yet how like home it seemed when I walked down
out of the unfenced hills, thirsty, footsore,
with words of greeting for the fisherman.

THE DREAM OF ARRIVAL

Awake, I did not know the land
surrounding me: the rocky coves,
sun shimmering off marble sand,
the cypresses and mourning doves.

Stunned by it all, I stared. Around
were cliffs I felt I should have known—
but for doves and waters not a sound,
no highway, house or telephone.

A stranger, eyes behind his shades,
greeted me in words I knew
as I half-knew these sunny glades,
yet by some instinct I withdrew

and asked what island this could be,
hid my longing to be recognized.
I gauged him as I would the sea
until he spoke the name I prized:

"Ithaka."
           Dissembling, I was home,
all I longed for so near at hand.
I saw Penelope, the loom—
then woke and did not know the land.

Always preparing to arrive,
I suffer the deaths of many friends,
survive, surprised to be alive.
My story's told, but never ends

❧ II ❧

The Collector's Tale

When it was over I sat down last night,
shaken, and quite afraid I'd lost my mind.
The objects I have loved surrounded me
like friends in such composed society
they almost rid the atmosphere of fright.
I collected them, perhaps, as one inclined
to suffer other people stoically.

That's why, when I found Foley at my door—
not my shop, but here at my private home,
the smell of bourbon for his calling card—
I sighed and let him in without a word.
I'd only met the man two months before
and found his taste as tacky as they come,
his Indian ethic perfectly absurd.

The auction house in St. Paul where we met
was full that day of cherry furniture.
I still can't tell you why he'd chosen me
to lecture all about his Cherokee
obsessions, but I listened—that I regret.
My patience with a stranger's geniture
compelled him to describe his family tree.

He told me of his youth in Oklahoma,
his white father who steered clear of the Rez,
a grandma native healer who knew herbs
for every illness. Nothing like the 'burbs,
I guess. He learned to tell a real toma-
hawk from a handsaw, or lift his half-mad gaze
and "entertain" you with some acid barbs.

So he collected Indian artifacts,
the sort that sell for thousands in New York.

Beadwork, war shirts, arrowheads, shards of clay
beloved by dealers down in Santa Fe.
He lived to corner strangers, read them tracts
of his invention on the careful work
he would preserve and pridefully display.

Foley roamed the Great Plains in his van,
his thin hair tied back in a ponytail,
and people learned that he was smart enough
to deal. He made a living off this stuff,
became a more authenticated man.
But when he drank he would begin to rail
against the white world's trivializing fluff.

Last night when he came in, reeking of smoke
and liquor, gesticulating madly
as if we'd both returned from the same bar,
I heard him out a while, the drunken bore,
endured his leaning up against my oak
credenza there, until at last I gladly
offered him a drink and a kitchen chair.

I still see him, round as a medicine ball
with a three-day beard, wearing his ripped jeans
and ratty, unlaced Nikes without socks.
I see him searching through two empty packs
and casting them aside despite my scowl,
opening a third, lighting up—he careens
into my kitchen, leaving boozy tracks.

I offered brandy. He didn't mind the brand
or that I served it in a water glass.
He drank with simple greed, making no show
of thanks, and I could see he wouldn't go.

He told me nothing happened as he planned,
how he left Rasher's tiny shop a mess.
I killed him, Foley said. *You got to know.*

★

You know the place. Grand Avenue. The Great
White Way they built over my people's bones
after the western forts made stealing safe.
Safe for that fucking moneyed generation
F. Scott Fitzgerald tried to write about—
and here was Rasher, selling off such crap
no self-respecting dealer'd waste his time.

I heard he had good beadwork, Chippewa,
but when I went in all I saw was junk.
I'm thinking, Christ, the neighbors here must love him,
the one dusty-shuttered place on the block
and inside, counters filled with silver plate
so tarnished Mother wouldn't touch it, irons
with fraying cords and heaps of magazines.

He had the jawbone of a buffalo
from South Dakota, an old Enfield rifle,
a horn chair (or a cut-rate replica),
German Bible, a blue-eyed Jesus framed
in bottlecaps—I mean he had everything
but paint-by-number sunsets, so much junk
I bet he hadn't made a sale in years.

You got to know this guy—skinny bald head
and both his hands twisted from arthritis.
I wouldn't give his place a second look
except I heard so much about this beadwork.
He leads me to a case in the back room.

– 39 –

I take a look. The stuff is fucking new,
pure Disneyland, not even off the Rez.

Foley's glass was empty; I poured him more
to buy time while I thought of some excuse
to get him out of here. If homicide
indeed were his odd tale's conclusion, I'd
rather let him pass out on my floor,
then dash upstairs and telephone the police.
I wouldn't mind if "fucking" Foley fried.

It's crap, he said. I tell this slimy coot
he doesn't know an Indian from a dog.
I can't believe I drove five hundred miles
to handle sentimental tourist crap.
He rolled himself upright in my kitchen chair
and looked at me with such complete disdain
that I imagined Mr. Rasher's stare.

I knew the man. We dealers somehow sense
who we trust and who the characters are.
I looked at my inebriated guest
and saw the fool-as-warrior on a quest
for the authentic, final recompense
that would rub out, in endless, private war,
all but his own image of the best.

Pretty quick I see I hurt his feelings.
He gets all proud on me and walks around
pointing at this and that,
a World's Fair pin, a Maris autograph,
and then he takes me to a dark wood cupboard
and spins the combination on the lock
and shows me what's inside. The old man

shows me his motherfucking pride and joy.
I look inside his cupboard and it's there
all right—a black man's head with eyes sewn shut—
I mean this fucker's real, all dried and stuffed,
a metal ashtray planted in the skull.
I look and it's like the old man's nodding,
Yeah, yeah, you prick, now tell me this is nothing.

He's looking at me looking at this head,
telling me he found it in a house
just up the street. Some dead white guy's estate
here in the liberal north allowed this coot
whatever his twisted little hands could take,
and then he hoards it away for special guests.
I didn't say a thing. I just walked out.

Now Foley filled his glass, drinking it down.
His irises caught fire as he lit up.
I sat across from him and wiped my palms
but inside I was setting off alarms
as if I should alert this sleeping town
that murder lived inside it. I could stop
the story now, I thought, but nothing calms

a killer when he knows he must confess,
and Foley'd chosen me to hear the worst.
Weird, he said, looking straight at me beyond
his burning cigarette. *I got so mad.*
Like all I thought of was a hundred shelves
collecting dust in Rasher's shop, and how
a dead man's head lay at the center of it.

I had to get a drink. Some yuppie bar
that charged a fortune for its cheapest bourbon.

I'm in there while the sun sets on the street
and people drop in after leaving work.
I look at all these happy people there—
laughing, anyway; maybe they aren't happy—
the well-dressed women tossing back their hair,

the men who loosen their designer ties
and sip their single malts—living on bones
of other people, right?
And two blocks down the street, in Rasher's shop,
a head where someone flicked his ashes once,
because of course a darky can't be human,
and someone's family kept that darky's head.

These genteel people with their decent souls
must have been embarrassed finding it,
and Rasher got it for a fucking song
and even he could never sell the thing.
No, he showed it to me just to get me,
just to prove I hadn't seen it all.
Well, he was right, I hadn't seen it all.

I didn't know the worst that people do
could be collected like a beaded bag,
bad medicine or good, we keep the stuff
and let it molder in our precious cases.
Some fucker cared just how he dried that head
and stitched the skin and cut the hole in the top—
big medicine for a man who liked cigars.

It's just another piece of history,
human, like a slave yoke or a scalping knife,
and maybe I was drunk on yuppie booze,
but I knew some things had to be destroyed.
Hell, I could hardly walk, but I walked back,

knocked on Rasher's door until he opened,
pushed him aside like a bag of raked-up leaves.

Maybe I was shouting, I don't know.
I heard him shouting at my back, and then
he came around between me and the case,
a little twisted guy with yellow teeth
telling me he'd call the fucking cops.
I found the jawbone of that buffalo.
I mean I must have picked it up somewhere,

maybe to break the lock, but I swung hard
and hit that old fucker upside the head
and he went down so easy I was shocked.
He lay there moaning in a spreading pool
I stepped around. I broke that old jawbone
prizing the lock, but it snapped free, and I
snatched out the gruesome head.

I got it to my van all right, and then
went back to check on Rasher. He was dead.
For a while I tried to set his shop in fire
to see the heaps of garbage in it burn,
but you'd need gasoline to get it going
and besides, I couldn't burn away the thought
of that weird thing I took from there tonight.

It's out there, **Foley** *said. I'm parked outside*
a few blocks down—I couldn't find your house.
I knew you'd listen to me if I came.
I knew you'd never try to turn me in.
You want to see it? No! I didn't either,
and now I'll never lose that goddamned head,
even if I bury it and drive away.

★

By now the bluster'd left his shrinking frame
and I thought he would vomit in my glass,
but Foley had saved strength enough to stand,
while I let go of everything I'd planned—
the telephone, police and bitter fame
that might wash over my quiet life and pass
away at some inaudible command.

I thought of all the dead things in my shop.
No object I put up was poorly made.
Nothing of mine was inhumane, although
I felt death in a kind of undertow
pulling my life away. *Make it stop*,
I thought, as if poor Foley had betrayed
our best ideals. Of course I let him go.

The truth is, now he's left I feel relieved.
I locked the door behind him, but his smell
has lingered in my hallway all these hours.
I've mopped the floor, washed up, moved pots of flowers
to places that he touched. If I believed,
I would say Foley had emerged from hell.
I ask for help, but the silent house demurs.

❧ III ❧

In the Borrowed House

IN THE BORROWED HOUSE

While flowerbeds have gone to seed,
a book you didn't plan to read
offers the unexpected phrase
that occupies your mind for days.

You write with someone else's pen
of someone else's life. And when
light's absence leans across the town,
you lay another body down.

THE SESSION

Two men at odds together in a room—
I the patient, he the earnest therapist
who exorcises my impressive gloom
in tones well suited to a hypnotist.

Slowly my fear unfolds wet wings and sails
over the blue carpet, the pillows strewn
like islands in a sea without details
where New Age music quells the last typhoon.

The exercise has worked. I yield him tears
and carry lighter cargo now. I'm free
until he starts to talk about careers.
Why, he wants to know, *insist on poetry?*

Why chain myself for hours inside a cell
when others only want my happiness?
He'd like to cure me. Eager to compel
another model metamorphosis,

he counters my ambition: *Let it go.*
I almost founder on his solid fears,
until uplifted by the undertow
of voices whispering for three thousand years.

ADAM SPEAKS

When I was clay there was so much to feel:
       symmetries of sunlight
traced within the feather and the leaf,
       pale secretions
trailing from shells, the clammy hands of fog
       touching my body.

My first uncurling into day was built
       from muted fires
below, and I began to grow distinct,
       bone, nail and hair,
muscled, akimbo, awkward as the fawn
       I later named.
There was a sea inside my flesh—I tensed
       to hold it in,
but found it was the whisper of the moon
       calling to me.

You who are thinking of me then, remember
       I tore my self
out of myself, bellowing like thunder.
       When I saw birds
I thought they were the love of God, and wailed
       at how they flew above me.

NIGHT SQUALL

That dream again: a boy manning the bridge,
the surging, Force Eight sea, the rolling ridge
raising the bow to clouds without a mark,
slamming him down to salt spray in the dark.

One lonely cabin light would keep him warm.
Imagining a refuge from the storm,
land out there like a hand upon the waters,
perhaps a family with sons and daughters

leaning in lamplight to their evening meal,
he lends their image secret powers to heal,
granting himself this gift, as if the earth
could give a damn about his daydreamed hearth.

He knows no better than a bobbing gull
the forces tossing him, how well the hull
will hold, how long the engine will secure
his progress inward to some sheltering shore.

But if he's lost his bearings in the murk,
with years he will learn a navigator's work,
steering from dread to dimly figured joy,
arriving, somewhere, like that bearded boy.

In king crab season, the cannery ship
trembled at anchor, its great boilers steaming.
The crew inside were soaked under raingear,
working the lines, extracting flesh from shells
with jets of water gushing into flumes.

I worked the crab boats tied along the hull,
long shifts in the holds, tossing live creatures
two at a time in the lowered mesh bags.
And when we'd cleared a hold and hosed it down,
a toke or cigarette took up the slack.

Above us they went on killing in thousands.
Guys we called butchers plunged their chain-mailed chests
down on the blades, breaking crab across them—
guts and backs in the grinders, claws and legs
packed frozen for the Lower 48.

We waited for the silence between killings,
when mesh was full of nothing but the sky,
to elevate our heads above a hatch
and watch the rain slant down through masts and nets.
Beyond were hump-backed islands under clouds,

as if a pod of whales, now settled in
to watch the people in their theatre,
were spellbound to rock and heather by the scene.
And none of us who worked there, none of our dreams,
could break the spell and bring them back to life.

BALLADE AT 3 AM

A Dunkin' Donuts denizen,
Phil diagrammed conspiracies
in which the country had a plan,
contrived by top authorities,
to generate our mass malaise.
When I would ask him why or how,
suspicion flickered in his eyes.
I don't know where he's living now.

Jake had the presidential grin,
describing all the Saigon whores
who sold their wares to a bored Marine.
Due to his unexplained disease
he lived on federal subsidies,
though late at night he would avow
his fate was fixed by a hiring freeze.
I don't know where he's living now.

The bullet piercing Marvin's spleen
was not a North Vietnamese,
but friendly fire from an M-16.
He wasn't even overseas
and bore no combat memories
that might explain the way his brow
twitched as if he had DTs.
I don't know where he's living now.

Lost in the disco Seventies,
I met them briefly, anyhow,
and went on to my girlfriend's place.
I don't know where they're living now.

Open the book of losses. You will see
that it begins with early morning light,
the stillness of a house where children sleep.
Not your own, unless love can make them yours,
they lie in their beds or in the crib upstairs.
The furnace breathes. Outside, no breath of wind.

★

No one commutes to work just yet.
No deer feed in the yard—as if
the world could breathe, just breathe, so still
that you might think it found repose.

A friend on oxygen is dying
in a city not so far away.
No doubt she lies sleeping now.
Perhaps her husband sits awake

like you, a cup of coffee steaming
on the kitchen table where he writes
like you, emptied of everything,
leaving his small tracks on the page.

★

You read of a man
without a wife
who had a plan
to make a life.

The Promethean spark
brought down to earth
served in the dark
new creature's birth.

But the creature walked
in pain, alone.
It wrote. It talked.
It prayed for one

that would not scream
at its ugliness.
It learned to dream
and to confess.

★

I think of that lurching creature even now,
watching a child whose smile and clumsy steps
delight the adults in the living room.
The sounds she makes are like the sounds of birds
during a downpour. She balances and walks,
reaching her mother's outstretched arms. Applause,
applause—enough to satisfy the soul
entire minutes with real blessedness.
When was it I began to feel this distance—
the self I dreamed of now mildly grotesque?

★

Oh yes, Nature, there is Nature:
the consolation of the trees,
birdsong again that calls you back—
delight of that first flight across
the desert floor. A window frames
the constant flutter of the leaves
within its stillness, green, enlarged
from what they were just days ago.
Breathe, just breathe, and watch them scatter,
held in their summer atmosphere.

★

given a watch
I knew the catch
hearing the latch
I watched the door
what is it for
if it closes fast
nothing will last
travelling past
all you adore

★

Each day you must cross from desolation.
You do this for no one, and no one else
will ever do it for you, foot by foot,
your body made of past lives brought to life,
each memory dispelled or trembled over
as you drive to work, or spend a day off
watching the school of leaves beyond the glass.

Do not expect so much, they seem to say.
The joy you've lost is only seasonal.
You must be patient. Start again. Small steps
will have to do now for the awkward creature
that you are. The child you watch, though not your own,
will teach you never to presume of life.

★

A deer steps, light as a breath, from the wood,
flickers across the morning-stippled road
and leaps into shade like a brown trout in a pool.
A yellow bus takes children down to school.
The mug of coffee on the open book
trembles slightly when a rumbling truck
ascends the hill outside. You listen, then
get up from the kitchen chair and cap your pen.

★

Never mind that we are dying.
The only purpose of the song
is to stop the baby's crying.
She'll not be a child for long.

Watch the infant cross the carpet.
Watch the young girl learn to dance.
She's on her own—you cannot stop it,
saving her from choice and chance.

Never mind the grief that wakes you.
Think of the alternative
where every kind of touch forsakes you.
Stop lamenting now, and live.

★

over the city where the friend is dying
over the suburbs a red-tail is flying
over the freeway throbbing at rush hour
over the ponytail prairie shower
brushing gray shadows across the long grass
and over the hills and the mountain pass

over and over the mind circles back
bending the branch that covers the track
the red-tail above you wheeling in flight
day becomes night becomes day becomes night

❧ IV ❧

Swimmers on the Shore

A MEANING MADE OF TREES
from a phrase by Seamus Heaney

This bedroom high in the old house,
its roof pitched steeply overhead,

traps the lakewater sounds, afloat
on what it holds: liquid lapping.

I could lie here half the day long,
hearing rain wrung out of the sky,

windows open, so the outer
breath and green of the world get in.

The alder's scabbed, serrated leaves
that will fail later in the fall

fulfill themselves, a waterfall
steeped in the greening chlorophyll.

That stir of limbs against the roof
must be the native Douglas fir—

a winter friend because it keeps
the housebound memory evergreen.

Most of all the cedar rises,
huge and straight, the hulking host

and omphalos of my dream world,
its rootedness a kind of triumph.

THE LOST HOUSE

A neighbor girl went with me near the creek,
entered the new house they were building there
with studs half-covered. Alone in summer dark,
we sat together on the plywood floor.

The shy way I contrived it, my right hand
slipped insinuatingly beneath her blouse
in new maneuvers, further than I planned.
I thought we floated in that almost-house.

Afraid of what might happen, or just afraid,
I stopped. She stood and brushed the sawdust off.
Fifteen that summer, we knew we could have strayed.
Now, if I saw it in a photograph,

I couldn't tell you where that new house stood.
One night the timbered hillside thundered down
like a dozen freight trains, crashing in a flood
that splintered walls and made the owners run.

By then I had been married and divorced.
The girl I reached for in unfinished walls
had moved away as if by nature's course.
The house was gone. Under quiet hills

the creek had cut new banks, left silt in bars
that sprouted alder scrub. No one would know,
cruising the dead-end road beneath the stars,
how we had trespassed there so long ago.

THE PICKETWIRE

Call back the summer as it stood so still—
whatever your sore eyes and tired pores will
of foxtail barley, fireweed, sedge and thistle.

A river cowboys called the Picketwire,
because of the way it braided waters tighter,
ground its round pebbles past a low campfire

where fresh-caught trout were browning in a pan
and you were standing, radiant in sun.
Remember this, and you are overrun.

A second nature rises from the past,
just like the first in that it will not last,
and grips you as it slips free of your grasp.

A MOUNTAIN SAXIFRAGE
Boykinia jamesii

James, I know, is for the botanist
who joined the expedition west,
but why *Boykinia*, I wonder?

Kin to the boy who climbs
the Braille of the granite face
in sunlight, before thunder?

Whose movements are like rhymes
in an unexpected place.
Who finds

the spreading flower
leaning from a cleft,
protected from the winds,

and knows
that where it grows a crevice
opens for piton and hex a forearm higher.

He moves now like a graceful thought
but does not think of what is left
by the bloom's roots—

cause of the great rock's slow decay
that with the coming snows
and the sudden heat of day

begins to rot
the very universe
he climbs upon.

A dance in what
was never really there,
a name, a breath of air.

A BIRTHDAY

Dawn of a sort,
and winter, and I
am forty-five,
alive in a landscape
I should have memorized,
where tourist throngs
of piñon jays
feed in the scrub,
and a rancher's cat
scratches my door.
Otherwise, silence
and this fooling mood.

At such moments,
the light indecisive
on peaks and valley,
one turns to the published
comfort of maps,
each thumbprinted mountain
measured, climbed
and claimed...

          Mapmaker,
what are the names
your names have erased?
What is the language
this land would be known by?
My grandfather lived
in Santíssima Trinidad
over the pass,
and here I find streams
called Mapache, Urraca,
the cordillera's color
a green-blue, saguache.

If I could hold
this early light,
this moment before
the defining sun
could stake its claim
on the dry valley,
this space between breaths

when the elk return
to their hiding places,
sagrada arena,
salvia or sage,
and snow before melting,
roads before traffic
of pickups and buses,
hold it in ink
that bleeds from my bones
on whispering paper,
horas de la vida
from Little Ute Creek
to Conejo, Culebra,
Kit Carson and Crestone,
the land grant to Spaniards,
Cabeza de Vaca,
before the Ute
and Comanche at war
for the gifts of this valley,
the bison and antelope,
yucca and yampa—
if I could name them
anew the first morning...

But the moment is wiser
than all my musings
and dies uncomplaining.

Somewhere a pickup
grumbles to life,
the frost on its windshield
touched by cold sunlight.
The deer go in hiding.

My duffle is packed
for the trip to the city.
My coffee has cooled
while I have been writing
through dawn of a sort,
in winter, as I
become forty-five.

MR. LOUDEN AND THE ANTELOPE

Mr. Louden was my father's ranching friend
whose pick-up sprouted rust from summer hail.
It didn't bother him. He had one arm,
and a tucked in sleeve, and drove us toward the end
of his fence line, passing piñon and chaparral.
Forty years. By now he's bought the farm.

I can still hear him chuckling: *No, there ain't*
nothing funnier than a one-armed man
driving while he tries to swat horseflies.
I never heard him utter a complaint.
He could have been weathered sandstone, deadpan
when his empty sleeve flapped out in the breeze.

He released the wheel to point as antelope,
like dolphins of the desert that were playing
in our dusty wake, surfaced alongside us
and in one fleet formation climbed the slope
ahead, and over it. They left us saying
little and were far too fast to guide us.

Where were we headed in that battered truck,
my father, old Mr. Louden, and I?
And was it the hail-pocked wreck that I recall?
Now forty-eight, I can't believe my luck,
to have seen those agile creatures chasing by—
unless, of course, I only dreamed it all.

Though I can't prove it's true, I saw them go
out of sight like figures out of a myth.
They left us gaping in their kicked up dust,
our own dust settling like summer snow,
while Mr. Louden laughed, conjuring with
his only arm, mage of the blooming rust.

A DANCE IN DESOLATION SOUND

Like wisemen treading water,
the black seals eye our hulls.
Sure he's safe from slaughter,
the biggest of them mulls
over the human sight,
thinks less of us, and dives
back to his briny night,
where, it appears, he thrives.

We push our kayaks on.
Our paddles rise and fall
in cadenced unison.
At the first good beach, we haul
our hulls and gear inland,
pitching a headland camp
above the tidal sand,
secure against the damp.

Such active rituals
make conversation spare.
We watch the herring gulls
ride the salty air,
and sense communion—
though we're not sure with what—
a father and his son
in this un-desolate spot.

But that is what we came for,
mutual solitude,
without requiring blame for
all we have misconstrued
or stumbled on, apart,
during our busy lives:
the lore of the broken heart
and tales of our ex-wives.

We turn in early. I dream
the wisemen of the sea
have flapped ashore. They seem
to be laughing at me
for all I do not know,
like my quixotic notion
that wisdom lies below
in the cold, cold ocean.

Awakened in the dark,
outside our tent I hear
the loopy, chattering bark
of otters playing near.
My father sleeps, but I
slip out into the night
under hushed summer sky
where animals delight.

Creatures of land and sea,
their arched, lithe bodies dance.
They take no notice of me,
but tumble down the slants
of rock to moonlit tides,
then frolic back to the top
for another of their rides—
a sort of Otter Hop.

What, if anything, parts
their sense of fun from mine?
They're masters of fine arts
learned in the stinging brine,
the universe of care,
of bigger and smaller fish,
where some survivors dare
to swim as they wish—

at least when they're at play,
and, playing, they are wise.
Knowing that my new day
starts with the sunrise,
I turn back to the tent
for an hour of fitful sleep.
Whatever this vision meant,
it will have to keep.

As my father turned the car into the drive
and we were home from our rare trip to church,
a man's voice speaking from the radio
caused us to linger there, engine running.
Just so, the voice with its calm cadences
lingered by woods where snow fell downily.

Though only eight, I thought I understood
the words to fit our snowless January,
and that the man, whose name was Robert Frost
(like rime I saw that morning on the lawn),
had died in Boston, which was far away.

Who knows where I went next, with all the woods
about the house to play in, but I recall
the chilling dullness of the winter sky
and firs so still I almost heard them breathing.
I thought it wasn't Jack, but Robert, Frost,
who made them live in such a cold repose.

Within two weeks another poet died,
her head in a cold gas oven. No poem
of hers was broadcast to my family.
Years would pass before I learned her name.

The old man in his woods, the young mother
dying with two babies near—such vanity
and madness framed the choices both had made—
the way he stuck it out, the way she lost it.

I've tried to cast my lot with that old man,
but something in her fate tugs at me too.
She can't have known the *cause célèbre* she'd be,
wanting to leave the world for leaving her.

The world goes on despite us and our poems,
snow falling in woods, or not falling,
lights coming on in houses, lights going out,
but I feel grateful that my father stopped
the car that January day, his head
almost bowed as he left the radio on.

SWIMMERS ON THE SHORE
Whidbey Island

Like half a filial circus act
splashing the Y pool shallow end,
I swam about my father, who could stand.
And when I climbed, an acrobat,
diving from his muscled shoulders,
they seemed as solid as two boulders.

Now I can hold his shrunken frame
in my arm's compass. We're together
on a park bench in lingering summer weather
before I make the long drive home.
But halfway through some story, speech
lies suddenly beyond his reach.

I see him cast for words, and fail.
Though talking never came with ease,
it is as if my father's memories
dissolve in a cedar-darkened pool,
while I no longer am aware
which of us goes fishing there.

Has he begun the long swim out
toward silence that we all half-dread?
I hug my father's shoulders, lean my head
closer to his, yet I cannot,
from his unfinished sentences,
quite fathom where or who he is.

I want to stay. The day is warm,
the salt breeze blows across the Sound
long plaintive cries of seagulls sailing down
to hover over churning foam
there in the docking ferry's wake.
I want to stay for my own sake,

holding the man who once held me
until I dove and splashed about.
He gives my hand a squeeze. There is no doubt,
despite his loss of memory,
and though the words could not be found,
it's I who have begun to drown.

A FLOAT

Flotsam? Jetsam? I don't know.
Not dropped from the jet stream
but floated from the Sea of Japan,
a glass float lost
by a village fisherman.

By the time I picked it up
in someone's summer house
it had already been found
on a Puget Sound beach.
The foundling I discovered was not lost

but left on a what-not shelf
among the paperbacks. I held the old
salty ball of glass ridged for a net
(that was not there) to catch
the long-gone fish.

The fisherman who lost it must
also be lost. The friend
whose house I did not find it in—
lost too in the sense
that dead people are

outlasted by a frosty glass ball
among dog-eared book jackets,
but not bested, not blasted.
Netless, maybe. Uncaught,
unreachable in this room.

1. In "Acrostic from Aegina" the word *Erotas* (accent on the first syllable) means "passion."

2. In "Pelicans and Greeks" some of the italicized words are quoted from Lear's journals and letters. Some are my invention.

3. "Towers of Silence": *Lariam* has been commonly used to prevent malaria, though some people (myself included) react to it with sleeplessness and mild hallucinations. I am told that some doctors consider it dangerous. As for the vultures of the Parsi towers, their numbers have been decreasing at an alarming rate.

4. "The Chambered Cairn": In Scotland graveyard plots are called "lairs." Ailsa Craig (Fairy Rock) juts into the sea southwest of Arran.

5. "New Zealand Letter": Darwin's statement was made after he experienced a major earthquake in Peru. This poem contains not only the proper names of some New Zealand flora and fauna, but also a bit of Maori and Kiwi. *Poms* are Brits. *Pakehas* are non-Maoris or foreigners in general. *Moko* refers to Maori tattooing, now common among gang members. *Hoons* are toughs or hoods. *Aoteroa* is the Maori name for New Zealand.

Grateful acknowledgment is made to the editors of the following periodicals where these poems (sometimes in earlier versions) first appeared: *The Connecticut Review, The Dark Horse* (Scotland), *The Dirty Goat, ELF, The Hudson Review, Metre* (Ireland and the Czech Republic), *The New Criterion, Northeast Corridor, The Ontario Review, Pifmagazine.com, Pivot, The Sewanee Review, Shenandoah, Solo, The Southwest Review, Tar River Poetry, The Texas Review.*

"A Float" was published in *Wild and Whirling Words,* edited by H.L. Hix, Etruscan Press, 2004.

"Kalamitsi" was published as a limited edition keepsake by Michael Peich of Aralia Press. "In Transit" was published in *Intelligence There with Passion,* a *festschrifft* in honor of Frederick Morgan and also printed by Michael Peich. More recently, Mike has printed *The Collector's Tale* as a beautiful limited edition chapbook. I am deeply grateful for his work and his friendship.

"A Dance in Desolation Sound" was performed at the Colorado College's Fall Convocation in 1996. The Colorado College has given me Faculty Development Time in which several of these poems were written or revised. They also gave me a two-year MacArthur Professorship which was profoundly helpful. I wish to extend a special note of thanks to my understanding Chair, Barry Sarchett.

A Fulbright Artist-in-Residence Fellowship in 1997 made possible some of the poems in Part I, and a long-ago Minnesota State Arts Board Grant also provided time in which some of these poems were written.

The friends who helped me with this book are too numerous to list, but I must mention Anne Stevenson, who cast a cold but friendly eye over an early draft of the book, and didn't object to my pilfering her phrase "bitter fame" in "The Collector's Tale." "New Zealand Letter" was written for a *festschrifft* celebrating her 70th birthday, edited by John Lucas and published in England by Shoestring Press.

David Mason grew up in Bellingham, Washington. His first two collections of poems were *The Buried Houses* (co-winner of the Nicholas Roerich Poetry Prize) and *The Country I Remember* (winner of the Alice Fay Di Castagnola Award). With Mark Jarman he edited *Rebel Angels: 25 Poets of the New Formalism,* and with the late John Frederick Nims he edited *Western Wind: An Introduction to Poetry.* He is also the editor with Dana Gioia and Meg Schoerke of the anthologies *Twentieth Century American Poetry* and *Twentieth Century American Poetics.* His own book of essays, *The Poetry of Life and the Life of Poetry,* was published by Story Line Press in 2000. He teaches at The Colorado College and lives in the mountains outside Colorado Springs with his wife Anne Lennox.